WHAT IS DEMOCRACY?

Julie Haydon

CONTENTS

Rigby

WHAT IS GOVERNMENT?

Government is the **system** that is used to rule or **govern** a country.

Government can also mean the group of people who govern a country.

Governing a country includes taking care of the military, roads, public libraries, and public hospitals.

WHAT IS DEMOCRACY?

Democracy is a type of government.

Democracy means "rule by the people." In a democracy, the people decide how their country is run. The people do this by **voting**.

These people are voting.

Countries like Australia, Canada, India, Japan, New Zealand, and the United States of America are democracies.

The word democracy comes from the Greek words demos, which means the people, and kratos, which means power.

5

A democratic government:

- Makes **laws** and keeps people safe

- Makes sure people can get goods, such as food and clothes

India is a large democracy. It is a country in Asia with over one billion people.

- Makes sure people have **services**, such as schools and hospitals

- Makes sure people are free to live as they choose, as long as they obey the law

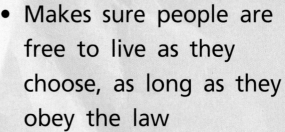

The Republic of Nauru is a small democracy. It is a small island in the southwestern Pacific Ocean with just over 12,000 people.

REPRESENTATIVES

Most democracies are made up of millions of people. In a democracy, most adults can vote.

Many decisions need to be made to run a country. If most adults voted every time a decision had to be made, it would take up a lot of time and money. So people choose **representatives** to make most of the decisions for them.

Representatives form part of the government. It is their job to **represent** the people.

ELECTIONS

Elections are held every few years. Elections are when lots of people (voters) choose a few people (representatives) to represent them.

People go to a **polling place** to vote. Polling places are set up just for the election. They are often set up in schools and public buildings.

Each voter fills in a ballot. The voter chooses which representative they want in government. The voter then puts the ballot in a special box. Votes are kept secret. When the polling place closes, the ballots are collected and the votes are counted.

In Australia, adults must vote in elections.

In America, adults can choose if they want to vote.

TAXES

It costs money to run a country. In a democracy, some of that money comes from **taxes**. People pay taxes to the government. Taxes come out of the money that people earn.

PAY

Alice

Gross amount   Tax

$3000 $500

- 1 -

paycheck

gross amount

tax

324-

Hugo Enterprises

CK

r

Amount after tax

$2500

People also pay taxes on the land and buildings they own and the goods they buy. This money also goes to the government.

RIGHTS AND RESPONSIBILITIES

People living in a democracy have rights.

They have the right to:
- An education
- Vote (as an adult)
- Live freely
- Speak freely
- Be treated the same as everyone else
- Be protected under the law
- Get together to talk or **protest** about an issue

This boy is obeying the road rules.

People living in a democracy have **responsibilities**.

They have the responsibility to:

- Obey laws and rules
- Vote (as an adult)
- Pay taxes
- Respect the rights of others

Imagine if you lived in a country without rights and responsibilities. You might not be able to:
- Go to school
- Wear what you want
- Choose your religion
- Choose your friends
- Play games or the sports you like

In a democracy, the government tries to keep people safe, healthy, and happy.

This police officer is keeping the crowd safe.

THE FIRST DEMOCRACY

Democracy began in Greece over 2,500 years ago. Men met to speak and vote on how to run the city.

Back then, there were thousands, not millions, of men. This meant they did not need representatives. All the men could vote on the laws and other important things, such as whether to go to war. Women and slaves could not vote.

OTHER TYPES OF GOVERNMENT

Democracy is not the only type of government.

In a monarchy, a king or queen (a monarch) rules. A monarch is not elected by the people.

In a dictatorship, one person (a dictator) rules. A dictator is not elected by the people.

In an oligarchy, a small group of people (oligarchs) rule. Oligarchs are not elected by the people.

Nepal was a monarchy. King Birendra and Queen Aishwarya of Nepal ruled their country until 1990. Today, Nepal is a democracy.

If there was no government, there would be anarchy. There would be no laws. People would have no rights or responsibilities. There would be confusion and disorder.

WORKING FOR THE GOVERNMENT

Many people work for the government. Postal workers, police and customs officers, park rangers and soldiers are government workers.

Can you think of other people who work for the government?

A postal worker

A police officer

A customs officer

A park ranger

23

GLOSSARY

govern to control or rule

laws the sets of rules made by the government

polling place a place people go to vote during an election. (A *poll* means the counting of votes.)

protest to let people know that you are unhappy about something. Sometimes people protest about laws that the government has made.

represent to act for someone else

representatives people who act for, or represent other people

responsibilities duties

services systems set up by the government to help people in their daily lives

system a way of doing something

taxes money that people must pay to the government. The money comes out of what people earn, own, and buy.

voting choosing between two or more choices. People can vote by raising their hands or by writing on a piece of paper and putting it in a box.

INDEX